Tutti Frutti

Jordan Jam

Dedication

I dedicate this book to my son Jae and my step daughters Analeigh and Mckinley. I love you all so much and I couldn't ask for more in life then being your mother. You all are such great siblings to Jordan and he is so lucky to have you all.

Acknowledgement

Thanks to my wonderful blended family that I get to write these adventurous and exciting books.

There lived a little boy named Jae. He was six years old and his favorite ice cream was tutti-frutti. This is the story how he came to like Tutti-frutti.

Jae had a beautiful smile inherited from his Korean dad and Filipino mom.

Jae loved his mom and dad a lot. It confused little Jae when his mom and dad were not together anymore. Little Jae understood later in life that sometimes moms and dads have to part ways for the best.

The big book called "The Life" is full of adventures and surprises, his mom always said.

Little Jae loved adventures and his adventures began when he met his awesome step dad. His step dad was not alone and has two beautiful Chinese stepsisters named McKinley and Analeigh.

McKinley and Analeigh were the same age as Jae. He remembered the first time he saw them all.

"I hope they will like me", little Jae thought to himself.

'McKinley and Analeigh! Meet your new brother.' His step dad introduced him to his sisters.

McKinley and Analeigh were thrilled to meet their new stepbrother.

'Mom, are these my sisters?' Jae asked

'Of course, honey! And from now on they are going to live with us.' Mom smiled.

"We can play all day," Jae and his sisters, screamed with happiness.

"Now that's what I called tutti-frutti," said his step dad, hugging them all.

'What's a tutti-frutti?' Jae asked his new step dad.

'My boy...It's an ice cream with many different flavors blended all in one scoop. Isn't that great? Just like us.' Dad explained.

That was the day when tutti-frutti became Jae's favorite ice cream.

One day the whole blended family planned to go on a fun picnic. They planned a hot-air balloon ride. Mom baked delicious chocolate chip cookies. Jae and his sisters loved chocolate chip cookies. She also made many different shaped sandwiches for the picnic.

'Mom's sandwiches look amazing. They have so many different shapes.' McKinley said and before mom could say anything, Jae jumped in and said,

'That's because the sandwiches are tutti-frutti too!'

They all laughed at Jae's smart explanation.

They head for the park after that. When they arrived at the park, Dad made sure a giant air balloon was ready for everyone to ride.

It was an exciting day for all of them. Jae took his favorite toy dinosaur while McKinley and Analeigh grabbed their plush dolls. Everybody was ready for the giant balloon ride. They flew above the beautiful forests filled with huge wild flowers and waterfalls.

All of a sudden, a strong wind began to blow across the sky.

'Oh NO!' cried the kids.

The strong wind grabbed Jae's dinosaur and plush dolls of

McKinley and Analeigh.

'Noooo...Our toys...' Kids began to cry.

Dad saw their toys flying pass them and said,

'Don't worry kids. I'll bring back those toys while you enjoy

your treats.'

They looked at dad who was lowering the balloon. Mom called them,

'Kids! Let's have cookies while dad is saving your toys.', said the mom.

Mom opened the basket and the delicious smell of cookies made them hungry. They grabbed the basket and ate all the cookies.

Dad slowly lowered the balloon and bravely rescued the dinosaur and the two dolls.

"Yayyy!!!!!", all the kids jumped with happiness.

Jae hugged his toy dinosaur. He also hugged his new Chinese step dad with a heart full of love.

"Group hug kids..." dad opened his arms wide and hugged all three of them while they laugh.

That day was a remarkable day because the balloon picnic trip made the bond between Jae and his new stepfamily stronger. They became a happy family.

A miracle happened later on and the tutti-frutti blended family was gifted with another flavor. A baby brother, Jordan was born. Jae, McKinley and Analeigh together watched mom and dad holding the little baby.

They all held his cute little fingers.

"I have an awesome blended family, American Chinese sisters and a Filipino Chinese baby brother." Jae said with a face full of smiles.

"And we have a Korean Filipino brother and a Chinese Filipino baby brother" McKinley and Analeigh said while running around happily.

"We are all one big happy blended' dad couldn't finish his sentence when all the three kids cried.

'TUTTI-FRUTTI FAMILY!'

Dad and Mom gave out a huge laughter and they took a picture to save the moment.